Dominate Your Divorce

Dominate Your Divorce

America's How-To Handbook for a Successful Divorce

Wayne Schoeneberg JD

Copyright © 2016 Wayne Schoeneberg JD
All rights reserved.

ISBN: 1539899616
ISBN 13: 9781539899617

Table of Contents

Acknowledgements · vii
Forward · ix

1 Choosing the right attorney · · · · · · · · · · · · · · 1
2 Keeping it Professional · · · · · · · · · · · · · · · · · 11
3 Fees · 21
4 Joint representation · · · · · · · · · · · · · · · · · · · 29
5 Leave the drama at home · · · · · · · · · · · · · · 33
6 Do your homework · · · · · · · · · · · · · · · · · · · 43
7 Discovery · 57
8 Children · 69

Conclusion · 87

Acknowledgements

I WANT TO THANK David Hamilton, Esq. for his tireless efforts in serving as the editor for this book. David's insight, in addition to his command of grammar and the English language, made this book much better than it would have been without him.

Forward

YOU MUST BE going through a terrible time. You and your spouse have split and now you have to go spend money with a divorce lawyer. And you know, or at least suspect, that the lawyer is more interested in how much of your money he or she can put into their pocket than what can be done for you.

I get it. As an attorney for more than forty years I am shocked when I look at what is happening in the family law arena. Lawyers are charging outrageous fees, judges are not hearing cases, or sometimes not even showing up for court and you, you want to get the best result you can but don't really know how to go about it.

If you have children it makes it even more critical, more complicated and more expensive. Many times you may feel like nobody is really listening to what you have to say. Your future is at risk here. Don't be a victim of your circumstances. Dominate Your Divorce.

Get More, Pay Less

This book is designed just for you. When you are done reading this book you will know how to Dominate Your Divorce. You will learn the ins and outs of what is probably going to happen and most importantly you will learn how to deal effectively and inexpensively with your attorney. The idea of this book is to teach you things your divorce attorney won't manage to tell you. What you will read here are the ways to get the maximum service from your attorney for the least price. Do not be fooled. You are going to pay something for an attorney. But if you follow the advice in this book, you should not have to pay more than necessary and will probably save yourself a lot of unnecessary anxiety and far more than the few bucks you spent on this very informative handbook.

Not Legal Advice

Keep in mind, there is no specific legal advice in this book. You should only get your legal advice from your own personal attorney. I will tell you how to go about that without spending a ton of money. But I am not your attorney and do not pretend here to give you legal advice.

I will use the terms "divorce" and "dissolution of marriage" interchangeably. They mean the same thing in this book. I will define other terms as I need to. This book is designed to be an easy to read handbook that will help you Dominate Your Divorce.

I know a lot about the legal system and how it works. I have been an attorney for more than forty years. I am recognized as a Top 100 Trial Attorney by the National Trial Lawyers Association and have the highest possible rating from Martindale Hubbell.

I know a lot about attorneys and how they think. I know what a lot of them think about their clients and it isn't pretty. And the good news is, now you have me on your side.

I am going to tell you some things your divorce attorney won't. It would be best if you are able to read this entire handbook before you select your attorney. That way you will be prepared to ask the right questions at your first visit. If your divorce is underway and you already have an attorney, set aside some time and finish this book before you do anything else.

When I talk about dominating your divorce I am not talking about how to win at a long, drawn-out, expensive trial. I am talking about getting what you want in the most efficient and least expensive way. That is how you dominate your divorce.

1

Choosing the right attorney

OKAY, IT IS time. Either you are ready to move on or your spouse has given you the news that it is time to end the marriage. Either way you are going to want to get an attorney. But you don't know any attorneys. So how are you going to find the right one?

There are probably attorneys in your area who advertise on television or radio. Maybe you have seen or heard some of their ads. Just because they are on the radio or television does not mean that they are good. It doesn't mean they are bad either. It is just their way of marketing.

Advertisements are really not the best way for you, or anyone, to pick an attorney. You need to know more about them before you even call for an appointment. I have seen some attorney ads that I consider to be misleading. You, the lay person, have no idea what it takes to be a good attorney. It is easy for an unscrupulous attorney to mislead you. The best way to do research about an attorney is to ask around.

Ask your friends. Ask your co-workers. Talk to your pastor. Certainly someone you know has been in a similar situation. They had a divorce attorney. Who did they use?

These are people who have had some experience in what it is you are about to go through. Their experience is not going to be identical to yours. That doesn't matter. You are going to get a lot of information from these sources. Don't just ask one. Ask as many as you can, time allowing. The more information you can get the better off you are. But don't wait too long. The clock is ticking. If you have been served with papers you need to get on the ball.

> This book is not legal advice. You should only get legal advice from your attorney.

If your sources say they had a bad experience, that is something you want to know about. Ask what made it bad? One of the first things you need to understand about divorce cases is that most people are not happy with the result. That is just human nature. But it isn't always because the lawyer was bad. There are other things that go into whether it was a good or bad experience.

People often expect to come out of their divorce in a good financial position. How can this happen? You are taking an entity (your marriage) that has been dependent upon two people and dividing it up. You probably had two incomes. How can you expect to maintain the same standard of living when there are now two people depending on the same amount of money and living in two separate places? You can't.

Ask questions. Ask a lot of questions.

What fees did the attorney charge? Did your friend think the fees were too high or did they seem fair? Remember that every divorce is different. Just because your friend paid $1,000.00 does not mean that will be your fee.

Lawyers charge different fees in different situations. Do you have a lot of property to divide? Are there children involved? Is there going to be a lot of arguing? Those are all factors that go into a fee for a divorce. There are others. But those are the first ones that each lawyer will probably take into consideration when discussing his or her fees.

You need to be comfortable with the fact that there is going to be a fee involved. That is how an attorney feeds her family, pays the rent and the staff. So if you think the fees you have heard are too high, don't bother to go see that attorney. There are good attorneys around who charge reasonable fees for divorces. Shop around but do not let price be the only factor in your decision.

I will explore attorney fees in a later chapter. There is much more to learn about that subject.

Ask your friend if he or she was happy with the level of service the attorney's office provided. Were the staff and attorney courteous? Did they seem to be genuinely concerned? Were phone calls answered promptly? This is important because you are going through a very stressful time in your life. Parts of your life are coming unglued. You should not be put into a situation where your attorney or your attorney's office adds to your already increased level of stress.

One of the biggest complaints I hear about lawyers is that they do not return their phone calls in a timely fashion. Something like that can be annoying. It is perfectly understandable that you would want to get a response to your phone call within twenty-four hours.

Keep in mind that lawyers are frequently out of the office for court. If they have a very busy practice they might not be in the office for the entire day. They won't have the chance to immediately call you back. But there is little excuse, although there may be some, for not returning a call by the close of the next business day.

If an attorney is too busy to promptly return phone calls he or she may be too busy to handle the cases already in the office. This happens a lot. An attorney might be insecure and take every case that comes in the door. That is not a good idea for an attorney. It is nice to have a lot of clients but there is such a thing as having too many.

When a lawyer has too many clients he or she cannot pay proper attention to the cases they have. The inability to pay proper attention to their cases often results in client dissatisfaction and poor legal representation. If a client becomes dissatisfied in the very early stages of a divorce because of a poor relationship with his lawyer it becomes extremely difficult -- and more expensive -- to resolve the case. You do not want be fighting with your attorney. And if you feel you are being ignored or you are not given the proper attention, it is going to have a negative impact on your relationship with your attorney. You are already in one relationship that is not good any more --your marriage. There is no sense in adding another one to your life.

The laws of supply and demand come into play in a law practice just like any other business. Each of us has exactly 168 hours each week to devote to work. A lawyer has only his time and knowledge to sell. What good lawyers do is raise their prices when they get to a certain point, or at least stop taking in new clients until their caseload returns to a manageable size.

So you are talking to friends about who they used for their legal matter. Ask them if they would use the lawyer again. If so, why? If not, have them tell you why not. You need all the information you can get. This is an important time in your life.

Another thing to consider is whether your lawyer is familiar with the jurisdiction. What is jurisdiction? It is the county where the court is located and where your divorce will take place. Each county will have its own particular rules about how the case proceeds during the dissolution of your marriage.

Depending on the jurisdiction there will be different requirements ranging from how pleadings and documents are filed, to when and where parties and attorneys have to appear. Is the attorney you are considering familiar with those rules? Does he or she practice regularly in that jurisdiction?

If the attorney has an office in one county and your divorce is going to be in a different county that could be a factor. You do not want to be tripped up by some obscure rule that your attorney did not know about. You also want to ask your attorney if he or she is going to charge you for the time it takes to travel from their office to the courthouse. If the drive alone takes one hour each way that could really cost you some big bucks! Some attorneys charge for travel time, others don't.

You should ask your prospective attorney how often his cases settle and how often they go to trial. You should really be looking to settle your case on the best terms possible without a trial. Trials are expensive -- and in most cases unnecessary. They happen when one side or both are being unreasonable.

Inquire as to how long most of his or her cases take to complete. There will be a general trend. Any good attorney has an idea of how long a case is likely to remain open. Having that knowledge is a sign of good fiscal planning on the attorney's part. If the attorney cannot quickly give you a satisfactory answer to that question, let that serve as a warning. You need to keep looking and keep asking questions.

Don't settle for the response that each case is different. While that is true, your attorney should have enough experience to know about how long a typical case will last.

Since you are going to interview your attorney before you select one, ask all of those questions and any more you think might help you. This is a process. You are hiring someone to take responsibility for an important part of your life and your future. Think of it as a job interview for the attorney. Keep in mind that there are plenty of good attorneys out there. You do not have to pick the first one you meet. The attorney is selling you something. You are the consumer. Treat this purchase as carefully as you would any other significant purchase in your life.

2

Keeping it Professional

THE RELATIONSHIP BETWEEN client and attorney must remain professional at all times and that is primarily the attorney's responsibility. There are rules of ethics attorneys must follow that go right to the heart of the attorney client relationship.

Everybody has heard about confidentiality. Your relationship with your attorney should be such that you can be totally open and honest about everything you tell him or her. Those conversations are protected by law. There are some exceptions but, unless you are going to disclose you are about to commit a crime you can reasonably rely on the fact that what you say cannot ever be disclosed without your permission.

Part of the reason for the rule of confidentiality is that the attorney needs to know the truth in order to give you the best representation. The rule of confidentiality gives you the chance to put all the cards on the table. That way your attorney knows what to expect and to know there will be no surprises. Lawyers hate surprises.

When I handled divorces I had a question I asked in an interview that gave clients some wiggle room. Usually clients are not willing, on the first visit, to admit to bad behavior or marital indiscretions. It seldom mattered that I gave them this nice, long talk about being truthful, clients want to hold back the bad news.

Sometimes it is as simple as them not wanting the attorney to judge them. Nobody wants to walk in and tell a stranger all of the bad things they have done. But an attorney would rather hear about all of the bad stuff you did than all of the good stuff. I never wanted to be surprised by some allegation of misconduct half-way through the case. Again, attorneys hate surprises.

If your attorney has spent the first part of the case telling the opposing attorney what a good person you are only to find out that isn't true it damages not only your credibility but your attorney's. The other attorney either thinks that your attorney is not prepared or knows you are not telling the truth.

Just because you tell your lawyer you did something that was wrong, or considered bad, does not mean the attorney has to tell the opposing counsel. Remember the confidentiality? Your attorney just needs to know.

So back to the question I used to ask. I would ask my clients what they believed the worst thing their spouse would say about them? That way they could alert me to something without admitting it. So if they told me their spouse was going to accuse them of having an affair, at least I knew to explore this further, later.

One day in about 1983 a woman in her early thirties sat in my office looking for representation on a divorce. She and her husband had two children and he had decided to file for divorce. We spent a lot of time talking about the particulars and then I got to the question. "Tell me, Linda, what is the worst thing that your husband is going to tell his lawyer about you?" She sat for a moment and thought. She had a real look of concern on her face. The anticipation was killing me. "Well," she answered, "I guess I really don't clean the lint out of the drier as often as I should."

I don't think I will ever forget that answer. The funny thing was that by the time the divorce was over it appeared that was the only fault this woman had. Her husband may well have been divorcing her because she was too good for him. The pressure of living with someone who was that good, nice, sweet, hard-working, and that good of a mother might have just been too much for anybody.

I have never gotten another answer even close to that. Honesty with your attorney is the first step to a good relationship. You should expect the same honesty from your attorney.

Sometimes the answer to my question was is not so benign. A man once told me that his wife would say he slept with her sister. Fortunately, that never came up in the divorce and I did not explore it any further.

There is a tendency for attorneys to sugar-coat their responses to client disclosures. I never believed in that and maybe that caused my business to suffer. If I saw a problem ahead, I pointed it out to my client. I always thought that was the best way to deal with it. Some attorneys do not want to confront their clients with the hard truths. I think that is wrong. If there is trouble ahead the client needs to know about it. How else will you be able to make an informed decision?

Another area where attorneys are not always responsive is giving updates on cases. The truth is that in a law office things can get out of hand. But sometimes the work piles up unexpectedly.

Discovery, which I will address later, is very paper intensive. Sometimes it seems the stars align in just the wrong way and suddenly a lawyer's office is covered up in requests for documents, interrogatories and depositions. Or maybe one of the lawyer's critical staff members comes down with the flu and it puts the whole office behind in the projected schedule. Some lawyers tend to panic. They will tell their clients something is being done when it isn't. They will tell a client a paper has been filed when it hasn't.

That is dishonest. It is wrong. It takes a confident attorney to look the client in the eye and say they are sorry but things are running behind. They should assure the client it is only temporary and that it will not have an adverse impact on the case. They should tell them that if it is true. You deserve the truth, good or bad. The honesty pledge must run in both directions.

Honesty is an issue in attorney fees. That is why you have to have a complete and satisfactory discussion about fees with the prospective attorney before you begin. There has been more than one scandal where attorneys have been caught billing more hours in a day than there are hours in a day.

The trust relationship is very important in this area. If you get your bill and it shows three phone calls the lawyer made on a certain day, you have to trust those calls were made. That is why you want to hire the right attorney.

Some attorneys may have you put money on deposit with them. That is not out of the ordinary. But that money is not theirs until it is earned. However, your money must be in a separate escrow account. If an attorney asks you to make an advance fee deposit that he will bill against, you have every right to ask the attorney to see the deposit slip where that money went into his or her escrow account.

I once had a very high-profile client who had a lot of legal business going on at any given time.

Some months my bill to him would be minimal. I would send him a bill and he would pay it. Other times his bill for just one month would exceed Fifteen Thousand Dollars. Now, this man always paid his bills on time. But I required that he deposit Twenty-five thousand dollars in my escrow account to secure future fees. That way if he dropped dead or decided one month he was done paying attorney fees I would deduct the balance of his bill from what he had in escrow and return the balance to him or his estate. But let me stress, that was always his money.

Make sure you get an accurate accounting for the money you have paid at the end of your case.

There is another area of the attorney client relationship I should discuss. That is the danger of having the relationship go from professional to personal. It happens. It shouldn't. It is wrong, but it does happen.

An attorney has to remain objective about you and your case. If you become too close the attorney loses his or her objectivity. It becomes difficult for the attorney to look at you just as he or she should, as a client. Suddenly you are a friend, or worse a lover.

Some attorneys like to take their clients to lunch. If it is a working lunch, (and I ask you, how much work can you actually get done about your divorce at lunch?) that might be okay. But this is a divorce. You have private things to discuss. A restaurant just doesn't seem like the right place to do this. How about dinner? Why does your attorney want to take you out to dinner, anyway? If it is for client relations, then I suggest you wait until after the divorce is over. Once your divorce is over, if your attorney wants to treat you to dinner, great.

See your attorney in the office. That is where your file is. That is where your information is stored. Treat your divorce like the serious business transaction it is. I have seen too many bad things happen, and usually to the clients, when attorneys start fraternizing with their divorce clients.

If you view your attorney in a romantic way, get over it. If your attorney makes a sexual advance toward you, get a new attorney at once and ask the one that made the sexual advance for your money back -- all of it. First of all, that attorney has violated one of the cardinal rules of ethics and you do not want to be involved with someone like that. Second, once you turn him or her down, that attorney will never treat you the same. You are going to need a new attorney and you will be starting over; you will need every penny of your money back. If you get in that situation and your attorney refuses to give your money back, you show him or her this section of this book.

3

Fees

Let's talk about money. Have you ever heard the term "conflict of interest?" When two people have competing interests, that creates what is called a conflict of interest. Lawyers use this term all the time. They cannot take a case where they are representing two people who have different goals. That is one area of a conflict of interest. There are others.

But there is a very simple example of a conflict of interest between the attorney and the client that boils down to your money. You see, in a way, there is a conflict of interest when it comes to the fees the attorney is going to charge you. He is going to take money from your bank account and put it in his bank account. He is going to do this by charging you a fee.

There are general rules governing the fees attorneys can charge and how they arrive at their fees. These rules vary from state-to-state. But generally the rules require that a fee has to be reasonable under the circumstances for the services provided. That is a kind of legal gobbledygook.

While one lawyer might charge $100.00 per hour for a service another might charge $400.00 per hour for the same service. Which one is unreasonable? Maybe neither. Maybe they are both reasonable. It depends on a lot of things. Certainly the experienced lawyer can charge more than the beginner. That doesn't necessarily make the experienced lawyer a better selection though. The less experienced attorney may work harder to satisfy you. Either way, your financial situation has to come into play when you make your choice.

It is important to have a very detailed discussion with your prospective attorney about fees. What is the hourly rate? What will you be charged for other than the attorney's time? Is there a charge any time you call the office? Is there a charge for copies? How much? Is that more or less than UPS or FedEx/Kinko's? Is there a charge for postage? Hourly rates and other charges should all be explained in a fee agreement letter you will get from your attorney. How much does the lawyer anticipate this whole case will cost you? He should be able to answer that question based on experience. If a prospective attorney does not offer to give you an engagement letter without being asked, that is a reason not to hire them.

A warning to you, though. You must be honest with the attorney about what you expect and what issues might come up. If you go in telling the attorney that this is going to be non-contested and you know, or suspect, that your spouse is going to make a big deal out of this, then the attorney cannot be expected to make an accurate prediction about the fee.

Some attorneys do divorces for a flat fee. A "flat fee" is a set price. You pay that one price and that's all. Many lawyers in the criminal defense field do that. If you have a traffic ticket, they will charge you $50.00 or $100.00 or whatever they think it is worth to them. If they have to go to court more than they thought, then they suffer the loss. If they get the ticket handled with only a phone call, then they come out ahead.

Unless a lawyer is absolutely sure that your case is going to be uncontested, I do not see how they can reasonably handle a divorce for a flat fee, unless it is high enough to take into consideration all of the possible contingencies. I do not do divorces at all. I did them years ago. Honestly, I quit doing them because people were willing to pay me more, and could afford to pay me more, to do other things.

Flat fees for divorces are problematic for me. Somebody is coming out ahead. One of the problems I see with a flat fee is that the attorney has made a business decision that he can get more business by announcing to the public that he will handle your case for a certain amount. He is doing that to get more business.

And here we go again with the question of how much business is too much business for any attorney? I suppose I could get all the divorce clients I want if I charged a flat fee of $100.00 for the whole case. I would quickly go broke and I would not have the time, anyway, to properly handle all the cases I would get. So, I would not do that.

On the other and, I might decide that it would be worth it to me to handle divorces if everyone paid me a flat fee of $25,000.00. How many clients would I have? Probably none. More importantly the person who could afford to pay the $25,000.00 flat fee would have a case that would require too much work to do it for $25,000.00.

> ... an attorney should know, within a few, how many open cases there are in the office.

If a lawyer or law firm offers to handle your divorce for a flat fee you are not out of line to ask them how many cases each attorney handles at any given time. Ask them how many open cases an attorney is assigned. I do not have a hard-fast rule about how many cases an attorney can handle at once, but if the lawyer says she doesn't know, or won't answer that question, move on. First of all, an attorney should know, within a few, how many open cases he has. It has a direct impact on the ability to spend time on each case. And your attorney has to be able to treat your case personally, not like a production line product.

That raises the question of who in the firm is going to do your work. I know that in the St. Louis Metropolitan area there are any number of attorneys with fine reputations for handling family law cases. But often the attorney is nothing more than the face of the firm. The work is done by associates or legal assistants. That does not mean you do not get excellent representation. But it does mean that the attorney who did the intake interview might not be the attorney who is going to handle the day-to-day work in your case.

You may go to a firm because of the reputation of a certain attorney. That attorney may see you at the initial interview. But then your case may be handed over to an associate for the actual work. There is a lot that goes into handling a divorce case. In a well-run office the attorney who has the big hourly rate does not do the routine work. That saves you money. You need to ask about that when you interview prospective attorneys. Don't be afraid to ask who is going to be assigned to your case. That is really who you will be dealing with.

Is it a paralegal or legal assistant? There is nothing wrong with that. But as the client you have the right to meet that person before you sign on with the law firm. The attorney you are meeting with may be an impressive individual. But her legal assistant may be a slug. And that slug may be doing the work on your case. So ask. Be empowered here.

If you are going to Dominate Your Divorce, you are going to have to start early. Your relationship with your attorney and the staff in the attorney's office is the first place to start.

4

Joint representation

One of the reasons you are reading this book is because you want to save money on your divorce. That is perfectly understandable. You are about to set out on your own and your finances are probably in a shambles. If they are not, you are one of the lucky few. The question frequently comes up about both of you using the same attorney. I never understood that concept.

You see there are few more adversarial court cases than a divorce. Yes, there are a few instances where there is nothing to fight about and no reason

> I think it is foolish to have both parties in a divorce case "represented" by just one attorney.

to fight. But think about the circumstance. Can everything really be divided perfectly? Are all the bills accounted for? If you can answer "yes" to those questions, then maybe only one of you needs an attorney. I think it is foolish, though, to have both of you "represented" by one attorney.

How can one attorney look out for the best interests of each of you? He can't. If there is a dispute, then he has to favor one side or the other. If you have both started with one attorney, you may end having to go out and get two new attorneys. If a dispute arises that attorney cannot ethically, or comfortably, represent either one of you. In my opinion an attorney who suggests or agrees to represent both of you is using poor judgment. Do you want to use an attorney who does not use good judgment? I hope not.

Papers have to be filed, time limits have to be met and documents have to be prepared. If one attorney tries to represent two people he or she is getting set up for a potential problem. You start out thinking you and your spouse can work everything out. You start out by agreeing how things will be divided. There are no children and somehow you have no debts. That seems pretty easy. So you go to one attorney and ask him to represent you both. He agrees.

> I think joint representation should be banned.

Then your spouse starts acting irresponsibly. He or she is late getting the documents that are needed, or leaves some important piece of property off the list. How can that attorney, who is supposed to represent you both, crack down on one of you? By then the attorney has learned certain things in the course of representing you both that he cannot use against you or your spouse. That is because he is the attorney for your spouse as well as you. In that case both of you have to get an attorney of your own and it can't be that one. So, beware of the joint representation trap. Some states allow it. I think it should be banned.

In the course of writing this I want to take every opportunity I can to remind you that I am not giving you legal advice here. I am giving you practical advice. Whenever you are in a situation where you think you need legal advice, ask your individual attorney.

Buying, or reading this book, does not establish an attorney/client relationship between us. That would cost a whole lot more than the price of this book. And just as important is the fact that I no longer handle divorce or family law cases.

I don't want to belabor this point but I can't state it strongly enough. If you are involved in a divorce, you need to consult an attorney. One purpose of this book is to tell you the things you need to know to find the right attorney and pay the right fees. You want to dominate your divorce. You need the right attorney without having to bankrupt yourself.

5

Leave the drama at home

THERE ARE A lucky few who get divorced without drama. They are rare. The dissolution of marriage scenario is filled with potential for drama. Notice I say "potential for drama." It doesn't have to be that way. The person you vowed to love forever is now going to be your ex-spouse. That takes an emotional toll in every situation and there is no reason to deny it. In fact, denying it only makes it harder.

Do you feel like crying? Go ahead and cry. Do you feel rejected? That is totally understandable. Are you angry? That's okay. Maybe you feel like a loser. I know when I got divorced I felt horrible about myself. I was the one who filed for divorce and I still felt bad about it. I thought my future was ruined.

I grew up a long time ago in a Catholic family. Catholics didn't get divorced. If their marriage was not working, they lived in misery. I couldn't do it. I decided I would get divorced. But it made me feel terrible. I felt like a quitter. But I had seen too many sad souls who stayed in broken marriages to know I did not want to live that life.

I know how bad you might be feeling but leave the drama out of your lawyer's office. It is just too expensive. Remember that every minute, every second, that you spend with your attorney or his staff is costing you money and precious time.

If your attorney has agreed not to charge you for the phone calls, meetings and emails your attorney is losing money and will soon come to resent you. If you are repeatedly calling him or her to talk about some indignity that has been visited upon you by your spouse, your attorney is going to tire of hearing from you. I know that doesn't sound right or fair. But it is just human nature. Remember all your attorney has to sell you is time and knowledge. If the attorney is charging for phones calls, emails and meetings, there is nothing wrong with that. Do you really want to pay that hourly rate to tell your attorney how poorly you have been treated by your spouse? That's what friends and family are for.

In most cases poor treatment and emotional slights have little or no impact on the outcome of your divorce. If your spouse is late picking up the kids for visitation, it really isn't going to matter. Sorry to give you the news. It does mean your spouse is irresponsible. But it doesn't matter that much to the judge. So when that happens, call your friend or a family member and vent to them. It is going to save you money.

These little indignities you suffer during the dissolution of your marriage are sad, frustrating and humiliating. They are irritating and unnecessary.

Do not let the fact that your spouse is acting like a child make you feel as though you have to act the same way.

The best thing to do is start a journal when your marriage first gets to that stage where you recognize you are headed for a divorce. A journal can be invaluable in helping you resolve your divorce. It will help you accurately remember things. That is important because your divorce could take more time than originally anticipated. If you have written important things down as they happen, you will be able to refresh your memory if needed.

> **Start keeping a journal as soon as possible.**

Having a journal will provide an additional benefit of giving you an outlet. A journal can sometimes take the place of someone to talk to when you seem to have worn out everyone around you. I have kept a journal for years. I find it very cathartic.

Keep a record of everything you think is important. Don't tell your spouse about it. If you do, you can be sure your spouse will try and find it and maybe even use some of the things in it against you. You should not ever mention it to your friends or family. People love to talk and before long word of the journal will get back to your spouse. This is your private journal.

Do not worry about spelling, grammar or penmanship. If your penmanship is bad, like mine, use a word processor.

A journal can be very helpful in your efforts to dominate your divorce. It is going to help you remember the important things that your husband or wife has done or omitted to do. It will help you sort out what is or isn't important. So make a record of as much as you can.

Start each entry by recording the date of the offensive action of your spouse. Then, in very concise terms tell just what happened. Keep the emotion out of it. Here is an example:

November 12, 2016 (Friday) Joe was supposed to pick the children up for an overnight at 6:00 p.m. He did not arrive until 7:30 p.m.

Or

July 20, 2016 (Sunday) Jane brought the kids back early and they had on the same clothes they did when she picked them up on Friday. They had not had a bath and looked very tired.

Or

May 24, (Tuesday) Mary said she would tell everybody at my workplace that I was a horrible father.

Unless your spouse is doing something that is an immediate threat to your health and welfare, or that rises to the level of a real danger to the children, just put it in your journal for later. When you meet with your attorney at a scheduled meeting you can tell him or her about the fact that you have a journal. Using your journal as a reference, you will be able to tell your attorney about these things in a very orderly and unemotional way. Your attorney will realize he is dealing with a winner and appreciate you even more.

If your attorney is interested in all of the drama in your life, he or she has too much time on their hands. That, or they are trying to jack up their fees by telling you that they want to hear it all. Most of these indignities that take place during the divorce are nothing more than annoyances. They are things that your spouse is doing to annoy you, or they are a continuation of a pattern of behavior that you once tolerated and now find offensive. They are not going to have much of an impact on the outcome of your divorce.

It is perfectly understandable to expect there will be drama in your divorce. I am trying to get across to you that you do not have to involve your attorney, or his office, in it. That will cost you money and quite frankly they will tire of hearing from you, even if you are paying the bill you get each month.

This is the type of thing your attorney will probably not tell you. Your attorney won't want to take the chance of offending your sensibilities and damaging your relationship. Your attorney may feel you are too "fragile" to hear this kind of thing. I think you are going to dominate your divorce and that you are not fragile. You are smarter than everybody has given your credit for and so I feel perfectly comfortable telling you this.

If your spouse has been cheating on you then your attorney should know about it right up front. Of course it is important. But you do not need to report every time you see your spouse out with the new love interest. By the time the divorce is filed it is clear that you two are done with one another. If your spouse has moved on, consider yourself lucky. Why would you want to be with someone who cheats on you? Let go!

I know it hurts. That is perfectly understandable. Talk to your friends about it. Make an appointment with your pastor. You might even want to see a counselor or psychologist. I am just telling you that you are wasting money telling your attorney about every hurt you experience during the divorce proceeding. Many spouses going through a dissolution of marriage "act out" in ways they never would have before.

That may happen in your case. Do not do it yourself. This is not the time to try and punish your spouse or show who you "could have been." Be yourself. There is nothing wrong with you. The fact that you are getting a divorce is simply a change of course in the journey called life.

You have to be strong in order to dominate your divorce. Start by telling yourself that you are on the way to a better life. You are. Your relationship didn't work. That does not make you a bad person. It doesn't make you any less of a person. Put it behind you and start looking to how you are going to turn all of this into the good life that you deserve.

Divorce drama is counterproductive. It does not help anything and it does not help your case. In fact, it harms you. You look less dignified and less sane. People do not want to be involved in your divorce drama, especially your lawyer. Any attorney who wants to be involved in your divorce drama should be avoided. They have little understanding of what it takes to move a divorce case to a successful resolution. An attorney who plays up the drama is playing to the crowd. He or she is spending your money on things that call attention to them, not your real issues.

There are going to be those divorces that you see on television between high-profile people who are fighting over infidelity, gambling, drugs, children and property. Their attorneys are in heaven. Those people have money they can waste and want to waste it on fighting one another. Do you have that kind of money? Do you have money that you want to spend on an attorney rather than on yourself or your children? If so, please send it to me. I am not going to do your divorce but if you are just going to waste your money spending it on lawyers, I am as deserving as any other.

6

Do your homework

When you were in school did you do your homework without hesitation? Did you bring it right home, sit down and knock it out, all of it, before you went to play? If so, you are going to love this part. If not, you really need to pay attention here. If you do not pay attention here, you are going to pay through the nose at the attorney's office.

If you are in the group that did not do your homework, or did not do it in a timely manner, you probably dreamed of hiring somebody to do it. There was this imaginary fund you could tap into and pay someone to do homework. Well, that fund did not exist then and it does not exist now.

The only money available to you is what you have now or what you are going to earn. Do not count on getting any money from your spouse. That may, or may not, happen. So, what is this stuff about homework?

Every divorce requires that the parties submit paperwork to the court. This is different in every jurisdiction. It definitely varies from state-to-state but it may actually vary from county-to-county within each state. The digital age held the promise of a paperless world. It didn't happen. We fill out more forms now than we ever did. They may not all be on paper but they still need to be filled out.

In almost every dissolution case there is a requirement that the parties fill out forms disclosing their finances. Of course, as you might imagine, they are called different things in different places. But the first one is like an income and expense statement in a business. Think of it that way. Your marriage is like a little business enterprise.

The first consideration is income. That is any wages, profits from businesses you may own or operate, alimony from previous marriages, that money you make on a regular basis by doing odd jobs, that babysitting money you make for watching the neighbor kids while the parents work, dividends from investments and interest from savings accounts. Income includes all the money coming into the marital business.

I frequently used to get asked about that "cash" money that used to be earned from those odd jobs. Does that have to be listed? Well, if your spouse knows about it and it is going in your pocket you can be sure your spouse is going to put it on the form. If you do not list it and your spouse does you can be sure that there will be a meeting with your attorney or staff about it. How much will that meeting cost you?

> **Do not neglect to list all of your income even if you think your spouse doesn't know about it.**

So my advice, (and **this is not legal advice**, this is *managing your attorney* advice) is list everything and let your attorney decide how to handle it.

On that same form is going to be a space for expenses. You need to understand this part as well. This is an important part of your homework. You must pay as careful attention to this section as you did on the income section.

One of the mistakes I saw people make was guessing about their expenses. That won't do. Your future depends on these answers. So it makes sense that you take the time to do your homework to have accurate answers about your expenses.

Think about what you spend for food each month. You probably have not really kept track of that. Do you eat out? Do you drive through McDonald's? You have to really stop and think about this. Many people underestimate that figure.

Maybe you buy your groceries at the same place all the time. Get in the habit of keeping your receipts. Now don't be silly and count your beer and liquor purchases as food. However you go about doing it, get some accurate figures.

Do you know what you pay for car insurance on a monthly basis? You better. How about electric, gas, water, sewer?

Another figure people forget about is routine medical and dental costs. Maybe you haven't been to the doctor in a few months. Or perhaps you don't go to the dentist as often as you should. Well, these are going to be expenses for you now that you are on your own.

People try to use the excuse that they don't know this stuff because their spouse was in charge of the bills. That won't do. This is your life. From here on out you are going to be in charge of the bills so you better be familiar with what they are.

Read these forms carefully. If you have trouble reading, then get a friend or family member to help you. Some of these forms are overwhelming. Many states are using the same forms they used years ago. They see no need to change them because it is the legal system and the legal system changes very slowly. If this is the way old Judge Adams did it twenty years ago, we might as well continue to do it this way now. That way the attorneys, clerks, staff and Judges do not have to learn anything new or make any adjustments.

Many attorneys have converted the old paper forms used by the courts in their jurisdiction to a digital form on their computers. God forbid they should have to go in and change all of that. Instead they just use an antiquated form because it is convenient for them. The legal system is not interested in making it easy for you.

The more complex it is, the more you need a lawyer. That is how lawyers make money. That is why you are saving money by reading and implementing the things in this handbook. Divorce attorneys are handling divorce cases to make a living. They are making a living by charging you money for their time and knowledge. They, like all of the rest of the world, want to have a comfortable lifestyle. So the more of your money they can get, the better off it is for them. Don't pay your lawyer or his staff to do your homework.

Some of the entries on the income and expense form are going to ask for weekly figures, bi-monthly figures or monthly figures. Wages are sometimes weekly or bi-monthly. Some of the amounts are going to ask for annual figures. There may or may not be legitimate reasons for all of this information but that doesn't matter to you. If the form asks for it, you need to provide that information and you need to provide that information correctly. This is important to the success of your divorce and it is important to your future.

Your attorney needs this information. Your attorney needs the correct information. But you should never have to use your attorney or his staff to help you fill this out. Do your own homework or get a friend or family member to help. This is one place where people get off on the wrong foot in their divorce. These forms are some of the very first you will have to fill out.

Your attorney will either give these to you when you retain her or will mail them to you shortly thereafter. They may come with instructions, or not, depending on your attorney. Read the instructions carefully. Read the forms carefully. Pay attention. This is your future you are dealing with. If it is too overwhelming for you, get help from someone who knows you and cares about you. Again, you do not want to pay your attorney or his staff to fill out these forms. That is a waste of your money.

The more complete you are on these forms the better off you will be. I admit that it might take more time than you thought it would to fill these out. If that is the case, then think about how much time the attorney or his staff will have to spend figuring out your income and expenses from the pay stubs and bills you bring in to them and toss on their desk. That used to always amaze me when people would bring in their income and expense forms with big parts of them blank or with question marks in them.

I would then have to bring them in, sit them down and ask them the same questions that their best friend could have asked them. When I was having to extract this information from them they were spending their hard-earned money on something they could have done for free.

One of the biggest concerns people have in a divorce situation is what is going to happen to them financially. Yet they will time and time again waste money on attorney fees by having the attorney or her staff do things for them that they could do themselves.

There is another dynamic in play that you might not have considered. Every good lawyer wants to get the best possible outcome on each case. Each case has a lot of variables. One of those is how good of a client they have. By good I do not mean how moral. I mean how interested is the client in helping to get a good outcome? When you do not do your homework, when you do not complete the forms you are requested to complete, you are sending a message to your attorney that when push comes to shove you are not going to be much help.

There is a lot going on in a divorce. Human nature plays a big part. Your relationship with your attorney should get off to a good start. A lot of that depends on you. Your attorney and his staff are providing you with a valuable service. But they do not want to be your nanny. They want you to take some responsibility upon yourself and help them help you.

You are probably going to have to fill out a statement of property. This will be a complete listing of what you own and what you owe. I want you to think of this form as a very important form. If you own something and you want it given to you in the divorce, then it better be on this form. If you own something and you don't care what happens to it, it still has to be on this form.

You see, it is all part of your estate. The court has the job of dividing all of your property. In most circumstances the division has to be "equitable."

That means fair. Now fair to you might not be fair to your spouse. Here is where problems can start to occur.

So let's say you have limited property or assets. And let's say one of those is something that you would never want. Maybe it is a sewing machine or maybe it is a table saw. Either way, it has a value. The only way to come to a fair distribution is to have all of the property listed. Because if you are going to get the $100.00 table saw in your column then you want the $100.00 sewing machine to be listed in your spouse's column. Get it?

No item of property should be omitted. This usually takes more time than you thought it would. But no item should be overlooked. If it has a value, list it. It may end up in your column or it may end up on your spouse's side of the balance sheet. Either way, if it has a value, put it on your statement of property.

I have been divorced and here is what I did. I asked my spouse to make a list of everything she thought we accumulated during the marriage. Then I took that list and reviewed it. If I did not agree with it, we would meet and discuss it. We would then come to an agreement of what was considered marital property.

Then I would ask my spouse to place a value on each item. Again, sometimes I would disagree with their value, sometimes not. (You are probably catching on here that I have been divorced more than once.)

Then after we agreed on the values I would ask them to go through the list and pick anything they wanted up to half of the total value. So if our marital property (houses, cars, bank accounts, furniture, etc.) totaled $500,000 they could take anything they wanted up to $250,000.00.

That way we would each come out with an equal distribution. Sure, that might mean they would have a chance to take my guns and leave me with that silly dresser I didn't like. But it did not matter because we had both agreed on the value. So if I had agreed that the dresser was worth the same amount as my guns I could sell the dresser and buy new guns.

In most states the court only divides what is called "marital property." That will have a different definition in different states. Your attorney will explain all of that to you.

When you are starting out to establish a new home there are so many things you need. Many times the things that are not listed on the property sheets seems insignificant until you have to go out and purchase them for your new living quarters. Do you have a mop? Do you have a broom, dustpan, garden tools, vacuum cleaner, snow shovel? Do you want to go out and buy new ones? Well maybe you won't get these things specifically in your divorce but they have value and should end up in somebody's column. If you fail to list them, you are cheating yourself. Your attorney needs a full picture of your assets in order to properly represent you. This is all about dominating your divorce and the way you do that is to make the best use of what assets you have while also preserving them. Your attorney is an asset. Use your attorney wisely. Give him or her the tools to help you and you will dominate your divorce.

7

Discovery

DISCOVERY MEANS INVESTIGATION. This can cover a wide range of activities and this can be where your attorney fees can skyrocket. That is why you want to pay particular attention to what I am saying in this Chapter.

Your attorney is going to need information from you. This can be bank account records, deeds to your house, retirement fund records and documents, credit card statements or other bills. It may mean that you have to produce your tax records. Do not waste time arguing about disclosing your tax return records.

The tax returns are subject to discovery if the other party signed them, and maybe even if they did not. Many times you will not have everything the attorney asks for. It may be that your spouse has the records.

If you do not have them, the attorney will have to file papers with the court to make your spouse produce these records. That is where your fees are going to increase. So, you should do everything you can to find these records yourself and deliver them to your attorney. It is better to spend your time finding these documents than to spend your money having your lawyer find them through discovery.

One of the documents used in divorce cases for discovery purposes is interrogatories. These are written questions from one party's attorney to the other party. They are answered by the party under oath which means you are swearing that the information is true and accurate. They can be a real pain, so get ready for them.

Here are some things you need to know about interrogatories.

There is generally a time limit for filing your answers. It can seem like a very short time, too. In some states it is as little as 20 days. That means your lawyer gets them from the other attorney, has to get them to you, then you have to get your answers back and the attorney's staff has to type them up and get you to sign them, all with 20 days.

If you get these in the mail, or delivered to you by your attorney, you are going to feel overwhelmed at first. That is perfectly understandable.

The first thing you need to do is sit down and read through all of them. Some of the questions may make you mad and you will ask yourself why you have to answer them? Don't start questioning that. If there are questions in there that are objectionable, your attorney will object to them. But it is not your place to decide which questions you must answer or not answer. Let your attorney make that decision. The immediate task at hand is to get started on your answers.

Most of the questions are probably going to be related to your finances. If you have been getting everything together as was suggested earlier in this book you will be ready.

Remember that you will be answering these questions called interrogatories under oath. The last thing you want to do is lie on one of these. If you do, you will be caught. If you are caught in a lie it will damage your credibility with the judge.

Why is that important? Well, if you can't settle your case, and most cases can be settled, you will have to have a hearing or trial in front of the judge. That judge is going to have to decide your future. If he or she thinks you are a liar, then you are not going to be viewed in a favorable light.

The reason you will want to get all of your answers completed right away is because you have to get these answers back to your attorney as quickly as possible. And if your answers are incomplete the attorney, or the attorney's staff, is going to have to sit down with you and go through all of the interrogatories with you to determine the answers.

Face up to the fact that these are going to have to be answered one way or the other. If you have to spend time with your attorney answering interrogatories it is going to needlessly run up your fee. Remember that the idea here is to come out of this horrible situation you are in and not be broke.

Another discovery tool is a Motion For Production of Documents. This Motion asks you to produce certain documents that are in your possession or control. These can range from property deeds and car titles to bank records, diaries, photos and any other document that may be relevant to your particular situation.

Once again, if you have them, get them together for your attorney at once. I suspect you are beginning to see that this whole process can be very tedious. These discovery tools are not used in every case. But you should be ready for them if they come. The more prepared you are, the easier it will be for your attorney to comply and that will keep your fees from skyrocketing.

If you accept that you are going to have to comply with these discovery requests, then your entire proceeding will run more smoothly. Remember that in most cases it is not your soon to be ex-spouse that is doing this. It is the work of the attorney on the other side. And, frankly, sometimes they just do it to increase their fee. Oh, they will say they are doing their due diligence. But I have seen many cases where all of this discovery is not warranted. So the last thing you want to do is fall into the trap of making a big scene over it and driving up your fees. Keep in mind that you want to dominate this divorce and the best way to do that is to keep your cool.

The last discovery device I want to talk about is the deposition. A deposition is when the attorney takes a sworn, verbal statement from a witness in front of a Court Reporter. Both attorneys are present, the parties are present, or can be in most circumstances, and the Court Reporter takes everything down in stenographic shorthand.

The Court Reporter charges a fee to show up, and the Court Reporter is paid to prepare a transcript of everything that is said. These fees vary from jurisdiction to jurisdiction but they are not cheap in any jurisdiction.

A deposition has a number of purposes. If there is a need for depositions, they are usually taken of the parties. So, your spouse's attorney will get to question you and your attorney will get to question your spouse.

The questions are all answered under oath, just like you were in Court. It is critical that you prepare for your deposition and here is one time when you should definitely meet with your attorney beforehand.

Here are a few things to remember. Keep in mind, I am not giving you legal advice here.

> **Please keep in mind that I am not giving you legal advice here. You must discuss this, as wells as everything else in this book, with your attorney. Only your attorney can give you legal advice and you should only look to your attorney for legal advice.**

That can only come from your attorney. I am not your attorney. You are under oath in your deposition. You should not guess at an answer. If you do not know the answer, say you do not know. It is not a quiz. The attorney is taking your deposition to find out a number of things.

One of the reasons for a deposition is to find out every bad thing you are going to claim about your spouse. So this is a good time to let go, if the right question is asked. But do not volunteer information. Do not give out information that is not in direct response to a question. If there is some terrible thing your spouse has done and the attorney does not ask you the right questions, do not talk about it.

But please remember to be guided at that point by what your attorney discusses with you, not what you read here. Your attorney is the only person you should rely upon for legal advice.

Sometimes the attorney will be taking your deposition to find out about something he or she suspects you have done. Please discuss this with your attorney. You cannot lie in your deposition. You cannot fudge the facts. So make sure your attorney is aware of anything that you have done that may be harmful to your case. Your communications with your attorney are confidential. Your attorney cannot disclose anything you tell him or her. But if they do not know about everything that may come up, you have put them, and therefore you, at a disadvantage.

Just remember that if your deposition is going to be taken, you want to be prepared. Be prepared to tell the truth. Be prepared by knowing what you want to say. Be prepared by not saying too much. This is one of those situations where you want to insist your attorney meets with you beforehand. I suggest you meet at least two weeks before your deposition to make sure you know what your attorney expects of you. That way you have enough time to go home and gather what you need.

One thing you do not want to do is send your attorney on a wild goose chase looking for things you believe exist, but that are not supported by any evidence other than your suspicions. I once represented a very wealthy lady who believed her husband had some funds secreted away in Ohio. He was always bragging that she would never find everything he had. We scoured the tax returns for any evidence that there were accounts we did not know about. There was nothing. We had an accountant look at their records. She came up with no evidence of any other accounts or any diversion of funds. Nonetheless my client insisted I go to Ohio and take the deposition of her sister-in-law. My client was sure that if her husband had any secret funds, his sister would know.

So, off I went to Ohio. I booked a flight to the nearest airport and then had to rent a car. There were no motels in the immediate area so I booked a reservation in a bed and breakfast.

The next day I took the sister's deposition. It took half a day to complete. I asked her every question I could think of in every way imaginable. She either did not know anything about her brother's finances or was so well prepared that she was able to hide anything she did know. The result was that we discovered NOTHING!

It cost the client a pretty penny for that trip both in my fees and the expenses. The client insisted I go. I had very little choice.

Here is something to think about. If your spouse has buried some money somewhere, or given it to a friend to hold, or somehow has it hidden somewhere other than a bank account in his or her name, you probably are out of luck. Sometimes there is just no way of finding that hidden asset. In most circumstances it doesn't exist. If it did, evidence of it would most likely show up on some form somewhere.

Discovery is an important part of some divorces. In others you can get through the process with only minimal discovery. But it is your lawyer's job to be fully informed about all of the facts that could have an impact on the outcome of your case. Make sure that you are dedicated to helping your attorney with this part of the case.

8

Children

DO YOU HAVE children? Do you love them? Then do not use them as a tool to punish or manipulate your soon to be ex-spouse. Children are little human beings who you and your spouse brought into this world. It is not their fault that you are getting a divorce. They play no part in it and frankly do not want a part in it. If they are old enough to take sides, do not encourage them to do so. Leave them out of the emotions and drama.

Your decisions are going to have an impact on their lives forever. But the fact that your marriage is not going to continue does not mean that their relationship with your ex-spouse needs to be damaged. That person you are involved in this divorce with is their parent. You were part of the decision to make that person their parent. You cannot undo that. So in the process, do not do harm to their relationship. It does not matter what kind of ill feelings you have toward your spouse, how badly your spouse has treated you or what a miserable excuse for a person you think your spouse may be, you cannot let your feelings for your spouse spill over onto your children. I promise you that if you do, you will someday live to regret it.

While you are in the process of damning your spouse to and in front of your children you are eating yourself from the inside out. Remember that this book is about dominating your divorce. If you are going to do this, you have to be operating from a position of full strength. You cannot be consumed and distracted by anger, hatred or grief. Nothing will plunge the knife of dissatisfaction deeper into the heart of your spouse (if that is what you want to do) than having the outward appearance of being in control and not falling to pieces. And if you have children your spouse is going to get a lot of information from the kids.

They aren't necessarily going to rat you out. But a parent can pick up signals from children that they do not even know they are giving off. So decide right now that you are not going to try and enlist the children as your allies in a battle with your spouse. It will cause chaos in the short-term and problems in the long run. Think about the big picture at all times. This divorce is going to last a relatively short time over the course of your life. But those children are going to have a relationship with your spouse all of their lives, or in very stark terms, until death do they part.

If your spouse has acted or behaved in such a way that he or she is a danger to the children, then your attorney needs to know about that. This is something that should be discussed right up front.

It will have an impact on how the case is handled and ultimately how much your attorney is going to charge you. You need to alert your attorney of anything that is a threat to the health, safety or welfare of the children.

On the other hand, just because you think your spouse is not the best parent he or she could be, that might not mean much in the divorce or in making decisions about custody of the children. The world is filled with lousy parents who have custody of their children. The courts are not there to judge the quality of your parenting skills as long as the children's health and immediate well-being are not in danger.

The two of you are getting divorced. The courts and attorneys pretty well assume that the two of you disagree on many things. Parenting is usually one of these things. Men and women who are in the part of their marriage where they are recognizing a divorce is imminent often say stupid things they really don't act on. For instance, some of them say,

"I will take the kids and disappear. You will never see them." Or there is a lot of, "I'll never pay you a penny if you fight me over custody." But the truth is that very few people run off with their children and there is always a child support order. Collection on that order may be a problem. But that is for a different book.

So do not become excited over the utterances about the children. But do try to take an objective look at how your spouse relates to the children. Would a third party -- a non-interested third party -- think they were a danger to the children? If you really believe that then you have an obligation to point that out to your attorney. You have an obligation to your children to point that out to your attorney. But if you just disagree with the way your spouse parents the kids, you are probably not going to get a sympathetic ear.

In many states there are programs that couples with children must attend before they can move forward with their divorce. One such program is called

"Kids in the Middle." If your attorney tells you that you must attend one of these, then get right on it. Get it done, past you and out of the way. Not doing it will slow down the progress of your case.

Family law judges want to do everything they can to make sure that the children come out of this divorce proceeding having a good, stable and loving relationship with both parents. And you should want that, too. If your attorney sells you a bill of goods about the possibility of significantly changing what is the typical child custody order without a very good reason to believe there is a basis to do so he is hurting you, your children, their welfare in the future and your finances.

Discuss your concerns, if you have them, with your attorney but do not exaggerate your complaints. Be honest and try to be objective. Remember that the criteria you should be applying is what is in the best interests of the children, not what you want to happen just because you want it that way.

Guardian ad Litem

Being objective is critical. If you do have a serious concern about the way your spouse treats or parents the children the court may take it upon itself to appoint what in most states is called a Guardian ad Litem for the children. And guess who pays for that?

A Guardian ad Litem is an attorney or professional child advocate who usually has some special training in investigating child welfare issues. So when a parent says that the other parent is abusing or endangering the children the court wants the objective truth. The current judicial thinking is that it can get close to the objective truth by appointing a Guardian ad Litem for the children.

The Guardian ad Litem will investigate allegations of abuse, neglect or endangerment and make a formal report to the court. The Guardian meets with the children, the parents and anybody else who has information that may shed light on the allegations. Does this sound like it is getting expensive? It is.

When you go in to your attorney's office and make these allegations, he or she is going to have a knee-jerk reaction to cover themselves from any liability by asking for a Guardian ad Litem. It doesn't matter to the attorney that the allegations are true or false, once they are made they can pass the responsibility off to the court who passes it on to the Guardian. Your attorney does not want to be put in a position of not having done something if your allegations are true. The children could be injured in some way and the attorney might face some sort of ethical complaint or civil liability. And the attorney has no way of telling if your allegations are true or false. So the default decision is to ask for the Guardian ad Litem to be appointed.

Now, it does not look good for you if the Guardian comes back and says that your allegations are unfounded. It hurts your credibility with the court and also with your attorney. That is why you need to be scrupulously honest with your attorney and yourself. Don't start making allegations unless they are real.

One of the things that courts are requiring now if children are involved is that each party file a parenting plan with the court. This is your suggestion to the court as to how custody and temporary visitation should be ordered in your divorce. This is an important document. The court and the attorneys will use this document as a roadmap to settling your case.

Everything you do should be aimed at making it best for everybody to reach a settlement. You do not want to spend all of your money on a trial. You can get what you want, or at least most of it, if you are reasonable. If your lawyer is talking about a trial from the very beginning beware! Most cases settle out of court because that is the reasonable thing to do.

So when you make out your parenting plan keep a few things in mind. One of those is that the mindset of courts at this time is to give the children the opportunity to have a close relationship with each parent. The "every other weekend" custody for dads which was the standard twenty years ago is almost never done in most jurisdictions now. Courts are ordering more time than that. It is not unusual for Courts to grant weekend time as well as time during the week.

I understand what a hardship this is on you whether you are a mother or father. I also understand that it is difficult for the children. I am not sure I even agree with the policy. But it seems most courts favor this arrangement. So you need to come up with a realistic plan. Your attorney does not know what is best for you and your children. You need to help him or her.

So sit down and spend some time on this. The best plan is going to vary depending on a lot of factors. Let me give you some of them to think about.

How many children are there?

How old are the children?

Are they in school?

Are some in school and some not?

What activities are they in?

How close do you live to the other parent?

What is your work schedule?

What is the other parent's work schedule?

How is the health of the children?

Do they make regular visits to the doctor for some illness?

How will the children be transported from parent-to-parent?

Are they all boys, all girls or some of each?

Keep thinking. There are bound to be other things you need to take into consideration. This is a tough part of the job but you are up to it. Do not give up on this part.

Be prepared to be flexible on these issues. Your attorney will assess your plan before it is submitted to the court. Make sure to get his or her opinion on it. This is an area where I encourage you to spend some time with the attorney. A good attorney is going to give you guidance here. And if you followed my instructions in the beginning of the book you have selected a good attorney.

Child custody and visitation can be highly emotional issues. Do not let it be that emotional for you. More time is wasted on this area than on any other. It is clear that you and your spouse do not agree upon things. If you could agree on things, you probably would not be getting a divorce. But remember, keep the drama down. Keep your feelings in check. Losing your temper or becoming emotional is not going to help you reach a solution. It will only cost you money.

Keep the children in mind. They are entitled to have a relationship with both parents. If you made a mistake and married somebody you now think is not a good parent, that is your mistake. Do not punish your children. As they grow older they are going to make their own decisions about both of you. If it looks to them that you unfairly interfered with their relationship with their other parent, you are going to come out on the losing side.

I once represented a very good man who really wanted primary custody of his children. He really thought it would be in their best interests to live with him. This was back in a time when the mother always got preference and usually got custody. She did in this case. The judge awarded primary custody to mom and my client was sincerely heartbroken.

He had some good arguments as to why the children should be with him. The mother was not a bad mother but she would never win any awards for her parenting skills. The children were 10 and 12 years old. They preferred to live with dad but years ago judges thought young children belonged with their mothers.

I assured my client that when the children got to an age where they could decide where to live, they would come live with him. And I was right. A few years after the divorce the father called me all excited. The kids had told to their mother that they were unhappy living with her. It also helped that the mother had lost interest in punishing my client by then. That had been her main motivation in demanding primary custody.

We filed a Motion to Modify the Divorce Decree and this time the judge did the right thing. He granted primary custody to the father.

As I said, times have changed. Years ago a father had almost no chance of winning primary custody of the children if the wife objected. But the current judicial thinking is to try and award joint custody of the children unless there is an overwhelming reason not to do so.

What that means to you is that you are going to have to accept certain realities. Pick your fights well. Remember that this is about dominating your divorce, not getting your way in every circumstance.

Be firm in your beliefs but be ready to listen to what your attorney has to say. Your attorney, if he or she is a good one, has your best interest in mind. It is an attorney's duty. Just because your attorney does not agree with every position you take, does not mean that attorney is not working toward your best interests.

Being a good attorney requires a certain amount of objectivity. The attorney should not become emotionally invested in the outcome of the case. That is where mistakes are made. Clients are not always right. But it takes a confident attorney to tell them that. If your attorney disagrees with you on a point you have the right to question them about it but listen to the reasons the attorney gives for her position.

Do that by having a dispassionate conversation. Here is what I suggest. Go home. Cool down. Write out a list of your questions. Look them over. Then go to your closest friend or family member and discuss them with that person. Do not try to sell your point. Tell them that you want them to point out the weaknesses in your position.

Then go home and re-work your questions. If you have done this correctly, you should have no more than ten questions. Write them out or type them on a piece of paper and leave space after each one so when you talk to your attorney you can take notes about what is said.

Your attorney will see that you are prepared and will know that you are serious. Do not just accept a "that's the way it is" answer. Make this a civil discussion. Speak and listen. Do not yell or cry. This is serious business. You cannot conduct serious business if you are emotional or upset.

I have had both men and women sit in my office and shed tears over their divorce, child custody, child support and division of property. Don't think for a moment that it is only one gender that gets emotional over divorces. That is why you have to keep your cool. The one who gets the most emotional is the one who wears out from the fighting and arguing. When that weakness is exposed is when the power shifts.

If your divorce has children involved that is the most important component. It is more important than anything else that will take place in that divorce. So this is an area where you really want to dominate and you do it by being rational and composed at all times.

Conclusion

Now it is up to you. The information in this book is here to help you dominate your divorce. Take what you have learned and put it into practice. A divorce is not something to take lightly. It will have an impact on you for the rest of your life. Make sure that is it a positive impact.

I am confident that this information will save you hundreds of dollars more than you spent on this book. But it will only work if you make it work. Follow the guidelines in this book and it will result in you having more peace of mind and more dollars left in your pocket.

If you found this book to be helpful I would appreciate it if you would take the time to post a review of the book on Amazon.com. Others in your situation may also benefit from having this book and they will benefit from having your comments.

I am a Certified Professional Coach and professional public speaker. I help people live the lives they have always wanted to live but didn't have the courage or confidence to pursue. I speak about second chances, self-forgiveness and hope. I do my work through presentations, consulting and coaching, publications and products.

Here is my web site: http://wayneschoeneberg.com

You can reach me by email at: wayne@wayneschoeneberg.com

You can learn more about me and the ways I can help you or your organization by visiting my web site.

If you would be open to a conversation about me speaking to your organization, contact me.

If you think you would benefit from becoming a coaching client of mine and learn how to live the life you always knew you should have or if your life hasn't turned out as planned, contact me. I have helped many people make a comeback from the pain, sorrow and feeling of loss that can come with a divorce.

Don't let your divorce define you.

www.ingramcontent.com/pod-product-compliance
Lightning Source LLC
Chambersburg PA
CBHW070101210526
45170CB00012B/678